Miracle In the Bethlehem Inn

A Christmas Play

By Mary Lou Warstler

CSS Publishing Company, Inc.
Lima, Ohio

MIRACLE IN THE BETHLEHEM INN

9358 / ISBN 1-55673-634-7

*To my sister, Decima,
who gave me the story idea*

Table Of Contents

Introduction

One afternoon when I was visiting my family in West Virginia, my sister and I were comparing notes on programs and plays which we had done in our respective churches — she as a lay person in a small church in West Virginia and I as the pastor of a small urban church in Ohio. She gave me several ideas which begged to be written. Out of that afternoon of conversation came *Miracle In The Bethlehem Inn*.

We used it in my church that year without scenery — only the imagination of the congregation. It was well accepted.

I hope and pray that others may find as much enjoyment as we did. More importantly, I pray that the performers may be able to tell again the birth of our Lord to a waiting world.

This program can be done with children, youth or adults of all ages, or a combination of all three. It was originally done with a combination with some adults (older adults) playing the children's parts. I find my senior citizens love to do plays and they like to play the part of kids.

"And she gave birth to her first-born son and wrapped him in swaddling cloths and laid him in a manger, because there was no place for them in the inn." (Luke 2:7)

Welcome

Prayer

Carol "O Little Town Of Bethlehem"

Scene I

Joshua, Miriam, and their children Adam, Lela, Lydia and Susanna arrive in Bethlehem where they expect Joshua's brother, Aaron, to put them up in his inn. They, like most people in town at that time, are there to be enrolled for the census. They arrive outside the inn. As they are talking, Aaron appears in the doorway.

Scene II

Inside the inn people are crowded around the large room which will double as a dining room/sleeping room for many. Marcus and Portia are there with their children, Claudia and Cornelius. They are rich, Gentile merchants who just happened to be passing through Bethlehem.

Scene III

The five children are gathered outside the inn on the steps. They, like most children, have had no trouble getting acquainted. They have had their evening meal and are just relaxing and getting to know one another. Talk leads to the Messiah. Joshua and Miriam appear and take the three younger children to the stable. Joseph enters with Mary.

Scene IV

The children are all in the one room, which they are now sharing. They will sleep on mats on the floor. Having difficulty sleeping, they are sitting on the floor, looking out the window at the star, talking about the night's events. Only Lydia is tired enough to sleep.

Scene V

The parents are all in the big room gathered around a small table where they're sharing something to drink and conversation. The children rush in with news of the Messiah's birth.

Scene VI

The families go to the stable to see the baby. They go to worship him as the shepherds did. Only Aaron holds back, believing it all to be nonsense. And then the miracle!

Carol "Joy To The World"

Benediction

Costumes

Joshua and his family are dressed as typical Hebrew peasants in the time of Jesus. Use bathrobes and towels for headdresses for the men and sheets or robes with shawls and scarves for the women. Headdress is discarded for scenes after they arrive at the inn except the last scene when they go to the stable.

Aaron, the innkeeper can also have a bathrobe, but maybe a little fancier. No headdress is needed since he is mostly indoors.

Marcus and his family are Roman in background so they can wear sheets draped over them like togas — the women's a little fancier with flower print or decorated with beads.

Any guests in the inn can be dressed either as peasants or merchants.

Mary and Joseph are dressed in the traditional bathrobes and blue sheet.

Scenery

Scenery can be as much or as little as circumstances permit. When this play was first used, no scenery was used. Only the imagination was invoked. The chancel area can be used for the entire play with a minimum of changes for the scenes. It is helpful if there are steps in the center area.

For Scenes I and II a doorway with the words AARON'S INN written over it can be used. Another doorway off to the left of the stage could read STABLE. These could be made from anything from large cardboard boxes, to old sheets which have been painted and hung to professionally made scenery of painted sections made by a carpenter.

There needs to be a large lighted star — either lit within the star or lit by a spotlight on it. The star can be made of cardboard covered with aluminum foil with a spotlight. A frame from cardboard can be covered with cellophane paper and a light put within it. You can even use a Christmas tree star. It should be hung over the place where the stable is.

For Scenes II and V, you will need only a table with four chairs, some sleeping mats, a candle on the table, some ceramic mugs.

Scene IV is the room where the families will be sleeping. It is a bare room except for sleeping mats on the floor and a wall with a window, facing the stable. If you want more scenery you can have a similar wall on the other side and a wall in the back where wooden pegs are painted and clothes are painted hanging on them. Light from the star shines in the window.

Scene III is outside the inn sitting on the stairs of the inn. The door is behind the children. If your chancel area has steps, they will be sitting on the steps, leaving room for the folks to come out the door. The star can be seen over the stable. If you do not have steps, have them sit on the floor outside the "door."

In Scene VI the chancel becomes the stable with Mary and Joseph and the manger. Now the star shines through the window behind them (or beside them if you can't get a window behind). Put a spotlight on the baby Jesus (a soft life-like doll wrapped in a white receiving blanket will do nicely).

Characters

Joshua   Father of a pious Jewish family

Miriam   Mother of the Jewish family

Lydia   Their very young daughter (about four or five years old)

Susanna   Another daughter (about 9)

Lela   Eldest daughter (about 11)

Adam   Son (about 12)

Aaron   Innkeeper — brother of Joshua

Marcus   Father of Gentile merchant family

Portia   Mother of Gentile merchant family

Cornelius   Son of the Gentile family (about 12)

Claudia   Daughter of the Gentile family (about 11)

Joseph   Carpenter from Nazareth

Mary   Mother-to-be of Jesus

Other non-speaking parts as needed/wanted (Scenes I and V)

Scene 1

(Congregation sings "O Little Town Of Bethlehem." Joshua, Miriam, and their children, Adam, Lela, Lydia and Susanna, enter down the center aisle as they sing the last verse. They have been traveling a long time. They are dusty, tired and their clothes are wrinkled and soiled.)

Joshua: We are here at last. Look! There is Aaron's Inn just up ahead.

Miriam: Oh, it will feel so good just to sit down for a while. But I just know Elizabeth is going to expect me to help her serve the guests.

Joshua: Well, my dear, we are staying here for nothing. You know how hard it is for my brother to make ends meet. I had to promise him something to let us stay.

Miriam: You mean you told him I would help? Oh, Joshua, how could you? You know how hard it is for me to travel. You know I am with child. How can I manage to help them — and with the children yet?

Joshua: I'm sorry, Miriam, but we have no money to buy a room. And it's not my fault that we had to come to Bethlehem. I would just as soon have stayed in Galilee. But what could I do? I cannot do the kind of work that Aaron and Elizabeth need. I cannot serve the tables and cook the food.

Miriam: You are right, Joshua. I know you try so very hard. And I am only a few months pregnant. I will manage. And Lela and Susanna are old enough to help. We will do the best we can.

Lydia: What about me? I want to help.

Susanna: Help do what, Momma? Will we soon be there? How long will we be staying? I'm hungry. When are we going to eat? Can I . . .

Lydia: I'm hungry.

Adam: Good grief, Susanna. Don't you ever think of anything but your stomach? And give them time to answer one question before you spout off with more.

Joshua: Adam is right, Susanna. One question at a time please. You and Lela will help your mother and Aunt Elizabeth with the kitchen chores and Adam and I will help with the stable and the animals. Lydia will come with us. She is too small to help in the kitchen. We must all be as pleasant as possible. Your Uncle Aaron has been very generous to us in giving us a room in his inn. It will be a very busy time and we must all help as best that we can.

Lela: I don't think Uncle Aaron is very generous at all to make us work like slaves just to stay a couple of nights here. But we will be good, Papa. Can we come to the stable with you and help there instead?

(Aaron appears at the door of the inn.)

Joshua: No, my dear. Your Aunt Elizabeth needs you in the kitchen. Look! There is the inn. *(Points to the inn where Aaron has appeared.)* And there is Aaron in the door waiting for us. Aaron! Aaron! Here we are! *(Goes to greet his brother.)* How are you my brother?

Aaron: Joshua! It is good to see you. And Miriam! How well you are looking! And these are the children? How they have grown! Come in, come in. Oh, by the way, Joshua, I am so sorry to tell you that the inn is all full. We have no more room. I don't know what we are going to do.

15

Joshua: What do you mean, there is no more room? You promised me a room for my family. What are we going to do?

Miriam: You cannot mean that! Surely you are joking with us! We have traveled a long distance. We cannot turn back. And the children are so tired.

Aaron: I am truly sorry, Miriam. But a very wealthy man came by looking for a room. Every inn in town is full. Mine was the only room available. Surely you did not expect me to turn away a paying customer?

Miriam: *(Sarcastically)* Of course not. How could I have even let such a thought pass my mind?

Joshua: That is enough Miriam. We will think of something.

Miriam: *(Voice catching like she is on the verge of tears.)* Oh, Joshua. What will we do? The children are so tired and hungry and I am almost at the point of exhaustion.

Lela: Maybe we can stay in the stable, Uncle Aaron. We will help Aunt Elizabeth and Adam can help Papa clean the stable and make it clean and warm for us.

Joshua: Lela, be quiet. You are only a child.

Aaron: *(Looking thoughtful)* She has a point there, my brother. The stable is fairly warm. There are some animals that need to be bedded down and fed. Yes, I think that will work out nicely. You and Adam can clean the stable and feed the animals in return for your night's lodging, and Miriam and the girls can help Elizabeth in the kitchen in return for your meals.

Joshua: I don't know, Aaron. The stable? Miriam is with child. I don't think it is a good place for her.

Aaron: Well, brother, it is the best that I can give you. It is better than the streets, is it not?

Miriam: *(Wearily)* Let us do it, Joshua. He is right. Even a stable is better than the streets when there are so many people around. You and Adam can clean one of the stalls and fill it with fresh clean hay and we will be warm enough. Come, Lela and Susanna, let us see what we can do to help Aunt Elizabeth get the evening meal ready. Lydia, you go with your father and Adam.

Susanna: But, Momma! I am so tired and so hungry.

Lela: We all are, Susie. If we hurry and work hard time will pass and we won't notice so much. *(Pulling her sister aside she whispers to her.)* Besides, if we are working in the kitchen, maybe we can snitch a few scraps until we are fed.

Susanna: *(Smiles)* Yeah! Let's go!

(Susanna, Lela and Miriam leave for the kitchen.)

Joshua: Come, Adam and Lydia. Let us go feed the animals and clean a place for our bed. Even a haystack will feel good to these weary old bones.

Adam: Yeah, I wonder if there are any donkeys there. I like donkeys. Some day when I am a man, I will raise donkeys and make lots of money. Then you and Momma won't have to work so hard.

Joshua: Keep your dream, my son. But for now, it will soon be night, so we must hurry. It will be darker in the stable and we dare not light a torch around the hay.

(Joshua, Adam and Lydia leave for the stable.)

Aaron: *(Speaking to himself.)* It is good to have a brother who has a smart wife and children. They will save me much money this night.

(Rubs his hands together and goes into the inn. Music — "God Rest Ye Merry Gentlemen" — begins to play and fades away when Scene II is in place.)

Scene II

(Inside the inn. People crowd around. Talking, singing, playing games. Marcus, his wife, Portia, and their daughter, Claudia, and son, Cornelius, enter. They are dressed like a rich, elite Gentile merchant family.)

Portia: *(Sounding disgusted.)* Really, Marcus! This is the most uncomfortable and dirty place I have ever seen! Couldn't you have gotten us something better?

Marcus: I told you, Portia, every inn in Bethlehem is filled up. Caesar is issuing some kind of tax and every Jew in the country seems to have come from Bethlehem. They are all here because they are descendants of King David. This is where they have to pay their taxes. Relax. It is only for one or two nights.

Portia: Well, I don't like it. And the room they gave us!

Marcus: What's wrong with the room? I think it is very nice.

Portia: Well, yes, it is okay. But, there is only one! For four of us! You would think that they could at least find another room for the children!

Cornelius: Yes, it is much too crowded there. I am going to ask the innkeeper to find us another one. I'm not going to sleep in the same room with her! *(Points his finger at his sister.)*

Claudia: Well, I'm not going to sleep in the same room with you either! Momma, can't we go some place else? This place smells. There are so many people here. And the food smells awful. Why can't we have roast pork? It would taste better than that stuff they are cooking in the kitchen.

Marcus: That is enough! We are here and that is that! There is no other room in the entire village of Bethlehem. I went to every one of them. And even some private homes have given up some of their rooms in order to provide a place for folks. We will just have to make the best of it.

Portia: Well! You don't have to be so sharp with us! Come children, we will find a clean place to sit for dinner. It may not be worth eating, but at least we can have a clean place to eat it.

(The three of them walk away with their noses in the air. Marcus stands looking bewildered.)

Marcus: *(To no one in particular — shrugging his shoulders.)* Oh, well. What else could I do? I can never seem to please them.

(Turns to follow his wife and children. Music begins to play "Star Of The East" as players get in position for Scene III. It fades when they are set.)

Scene III

(Lela, Adam, Susanna, Claudia and Cornelius are all sitting outside the inn — on low chairs or steps in chancel area if they are present. A star shines brightly behind them.)

Adam: Have you noticed the stars tonight? That one is so bright that Papa and I were able to clean the stable and get it all ready for bed without using a torch.

Cornelius: What do you mean, cleaning the stable to get it ready for bed? Isn't the stable where the animals live?

Susanna: Yeah, but Uncle Aaron gave our room away, so we have to sleep in the barn.

Claudia: Gave your room away? What do you mean?

Lela: Well, you see, Uncle Aaron owns this inn. He told Papa that we could stay here when Caesar said we had to come to Bethlehem to pay a tax. But when we got here, he already gave it to some rich merchant who could pay for it.

Cornelius: You must mean us! We took your room? But there are six of you. How could you live in one room? It is too small for four of us!

Adam: It is plenty big enough for two families! We are used to sleeping on mats on the floor. We only have two rooms for our family in Galilee.

Claudia: But, don't you get tired of getting in each other's way?

Susanna: Oh, sometimes we argue, but we really get along quite well. We have our fun feasts and play and cook and ...

Lela: Susanna! They didn't ask for a history of our family.

Claudia: But that is interesting. What is this tax that everyone is talking about? And why are you in Bethlehem?

Adam: Caesar wants to know how many Jews are under his rule. He wants to make sure that they all pay something to keep the government going. The easiest way to count Jews is by their heritage. Our father is a descendant of King David, who was born in Bethlehem. So we had to come here to register and pay our tax.

Claudia: But, if you had a King, why are you under Roman rule?

Lela: It is a long story. We had lots of Kings and they all disobeyed — or at least most of them disobeyed — our God and his commands. Our people were taken into captivity and God promised that someday he would send a Messiah to save us.

Susanna: Lela, why did you mention this Messiah? What does that have to do with anything?

Lela: I don't know. The thought just popped into my head. Maybe it is the strange star that seems to hang so low above us. Maybe it is just the trip here and all the people. It just seems like a night of miracles and I thought of the Messiah.

Cornelius: Who is this Messiah? Another King to replace Caesar? You could get in big trouble with that kind of talk.

Adam: No, No! Our Messiah, when he comes, will be a King greater than any king — even our King David — and your Caesar. We have been looking for him for many, many years. But, Lela is right. This is a strange night. That star is different. We have been oppressed so long, maybe this is the night of miracles and Messiahs.

(Joshua and Miriam and Lydia enter as Adam is talking.)

Joshua: What is all this talk about Messiahs and miracles? It is getting late. Come, we must get ourselves settled down in the hay while that star still offers us light.

Miriam: Yes, it is late, and we are all very tired. You can talk to your new friends tomorrow. Come, let us go to the stable.

Adam: I am not tired now. May I please stay a while and watch the star and talk with my new friends?

Joshua: *(Looks thoughtful for a second or two.)* All right, you may stay a while. Since you helped prepare the stable, you know where we are in case the star moves on. Don't be too late.

(Joshua, Miriam and the girls move off toward the "stable.")

Cornelius: You really are going to sleep in the stable? With the animals?

Adam: Yes. It is warm and dry. We will be comfortable.

Claudia: Is it true about your Messiah? Will he care about other people, too? Like us?

Adam: Oh, yes! When our Messiah comes, he will save all people. He will be a great King!

(Enter Marcus and Portia while children are talking.)

Marcus: What is all this nonsense about Messiahs and great kings?

Cornelius: It's true, Papa. A Messiah who is greater than their King David and our Caesar will come some day and all people will be saved from poverty and greed and ...

23

Marcus: That is enough, Cornelius! You know that is treason talk. We will hear none of it.

Adam: But, Sir, don't you want peace on earth for everyone?

Portia: Of course he does. Everyone wants peace on earth.

Adam: Our Messiah will bring peace to everyone.

Claudia: Speaking of peace on earth, look there! *(Points toward Mary and Joseph who have begun walking slowly down the center aisle.)* It is a man with a woman on a donkey. Surely they don't think they will get a room this time of night! We had to kick these poor people out to the stable in order to have a room.

Marcus: What are you talking about? Kicking who out to the stable?

Cornelius: Adam and his family are relatives of the innkeeper. They were supposed to have our room, but the innkeeper gave it to us because he needed the money. And he let Adam and his family use the stable to sleep tonight.

Portia: Really? We are complaining about a room which should have gone to someone else? Someone else is sleeping in the stable so we can have a room?

Claudia: That's right, Momma. Seems a little wrong, somehow, doesn't it?

(Mary and Joseph approach the inn.)

Joseph: Could you tell me where I can find the innkeeper? I must have a place to stay tonight.

Cornelius: Good luck! There ain't no more rooms!

Portia: Cornelius! There aren't any more rooms.

Cornelius: That's what I said. They don't have any more. We took the last one. Even the stable is full.

Joseph: But I must have a place to stay. My wife is about to give birth!

(Aaron enters as they are talking.)

Aaron: The kid is right. I don't have any more rooms. I don't even have room in my stable.

Joseph: But what will we do? My wife is about to have a baby and she must have some place to lie down. I cannot ask her to give birth here in the middle of the streets of Bethlehem!

Adam: Wait, Uncle Aaron. Don't send them away. I have an idea. Let me go ask my father. We will give them our place in the stable.

Aaron: You are a good-hearted boy, Adam — foolish, but good-hearted. Your father is no fool, though. He will not turn his own family out. Where will you stay?

Adam: I don't know, but I feel that I must ask Father.

Joseph: We have traveled so far. We had to come to register. We hoped the baby would be born before we had to leave. But it wasn't. I am afraid for my wife. She is so young and so small. The trip has been so hard on her. But she has not complained. I feel so hopeless. What will we do?

Cornelius: Momma? Papa? Could we give them our room?

Claudia: Don't be ridiculous. Where would we sleep?

Cornelius: We could go to the stable with Adam and his family. Then maybe when their Messiah comes, he would remember us, too.

Portia: You are too impressionable! We simply must get you out of this place!

(Adam returns with his father, mother and sisters.)

Miriam: What is this Adam is telling us? A young woman about to give birth to a child and you are turning them away? For shame, Aaron. For shame!

Aaron: Well, what can I do? I don't have ANY place. Every single spot is taken. Even Elizabeth and I are sleeping on the floor in the big room with everyone else!

Miriam: Well, I'm sure there is something. Yahweh would not have us turn away a poor mother in labor. They will have our clean stall. We have even prepared a manger with new clean hay for the baby. *(Goes over and puts her arms around Mary.)* Come, child. We will make you comfortable. God will provide a place for us. You must have a clean, dry, private place. I will help you get settled.

Adam: Where is your donkey? I will take care of her for you.

Joseph: Thank you young man. She is tied up over there. *(Points in the direction from which he has come.)* Please be gentle with her. She has been faithful and good in carrying her burden this day.

Adam: I will, Sir. I love donkeys. Some day I will raise donkeys. That is my dream.

Joseph: May Yahweh grant your dream to come true.

Mary: Thank you so much. God does provide. God has led us to you. And we are so grateful.

(Mary and Joseph leave for the stable, and Miriam goes with them with her arm still around Mary.)

Aaron: *(Sarcastically.)* Now that was real sweet of you — stupid, but sweet! Now what are YOU going to do? Where do you think you are going to sleep?

Adam: God will provide. He will keep it warm for us to sleep under the stars. But I must look after the little donkey. *(He leaves in the direction of the donkey.)*

Portia: No! I have not seen such great faith ever before! I must hear more of this God who provides and of this Messiah the children talk about. Come, our room is big enough for 20. Surely 10 of us can stay the night there.

(All the rest go into the inn except Aaron.)

Aaron: *(Shaking his head.)* Messiahs? Miracles? God? What is this world coming to?

(Turns and goes into the inn as the music begins to play "Away In A Manger.")

Scene IV

(Children gather around the window and talk quietly. Lydia is sleeping on the floor a little distance from the rest.)

Lela: Can you believe it? A baby was born right there in the stable. It sure is a good thing Adam and Papa had cleaned it and made it warm and nice. And the little baby lying there in the manger! He was so cute! I feel like there is something special about that baby. Does anyone else feel it?

Claudia: Yeah, I know what you mean. I have seen a lot of babies before, but this one is different. It is almost as if he could really understand us — like he could see inside me.

Cornelius: *(Sounding disgusted.)* Girls! You always make a big deal out of everything! He's just a baby — and a lucky one at that. A few more hours of wandering the streets of Bethlehem and he would have been born in some side street.

Adam: No, Cornelius, they are right. I feel it, too. I believe God is speaking to us in a special way this night. Something has changed your parents — and us too.

Susanna: Do you suppose that baby could be the Messiah? Isn't he supposed to change people?

Cornelius: I thought you said the Messiah would be a King. That tiny little red-faced baby sure didn't look like a King to me.

Lela: Well, yes, our Messiah will be a King, but even kings have to be born and grow up, don't they? And maybe Mary and Joseph are really a prince and princess who are hiding from the Roman government. Maybe they are really the parents of our Messiah.

Claudia: Boy, you sure do have an imagination, don't you!

Susanna: But, she may be right, you know. After all this is a strange night. Look at that star. Did you ever see anything so bright? It was almost like daylight in the stable.

Adam: You are right. And it became brighter when the baby was born. It was almost as if it were shining especially for that baby.

Lela: Shhh! Listen.

(Music begins playing very softly in the background "Joy To The World.")

Susanna: What is it? What do you hear? I don't hear anything.

Lela: Shhh! How can you hear anything when you are chattering so? Listen! I hear music — and yet, not like any I've heard before. Do you hear it?

(All are quiet listening. Music begins to play a little louder, but still softly.)

Adam: You are right. I hear it, too. It sounds like it is coming from the hill country over there. Do you hear it, Claudia? Cornelius?

Claudia: Yes, I hear it too! It is beautiful. Should we call our parents?

Cornelius: It will probably be gone by the time they get here, and they will just yell at us for not being asleep.

Susanna: I wonder who is singing. I bet it is angels!

Cornelius: And we thought Lela has an imagination! *(Scoffingly)* Angels! I suppose you have heard lots of angels before and know what they sound like.

Susanna: Well, no. But I still bet they are angels.

Lela: What are they singing? Sounds like something about "Peace on earth and good will to men."

Claudia: Maybe you are right. Maybe the baby is your Messiah. Maybe your God is singing the news to the world. I wonder if anyone else hears it. I wonder if we should go tell Mary and Joseph.

Cornelius: Come on, sister, dear. Don't get carried away. It is probably just some shepherds singing to their sheep. *(Music stops.)* See, it has stopped already. The shepherds have probably gone to sleep. And we had better go to sleep, too. It has been a long day and I am tired. *(Yawns and stretches as he prepares to lie down to sleep.)*

Adam: Yeah, he's right. We need to go to sleep. But that star is so bright. I'm not sure I can. *(Turns to look out the window one more time.)* Look! What is that? More people coming to Bethlehem? Surely not!

Lela: Let me see! *(Looks out the window.)* It looks like shepherds. See! They even have their shepherds' crooks with them. I wonder where they are going. Surely not to this inn.

Susanna: I want to see. I want to see. Look! They are going to the stable. Maybe they have some animals there.

Adam: No, there are no sheep there — at least not any that are unaccounted for. I'm going to find out what they are doing.

Susanna: Where are you going, Adam? You shouldn't go out. You know Momma and Papa will be upset.

Adam: I know, but I must see what they are up to. We can't have strange men going in there harming our baby, can we?

Cornelius: Our baby? Just because we made a place for them to stay doesn't make it our baby, does it? *(Cornelius stares at Adam and Adam returns the stare.)* Well, all right. So it is our baby. I'll go with you.

Claudia: Me, too. I'll go, too!

Cornelius: No, you stay here. This is man's work.

(Cornelius and Adam leave. Lydia wakes, stretches and comes over to the girls, rubbing her eyes)

Lydia: Where is Adam going?

Lela: Never mind. Go back to sleep.

Lydia: I don't want to.

Susanna: Who do you suppose they are? What do they want? Why are they here? Do you think they will harm the baby? What ...

Lela: Susie, you are asking too many questions again. We will just have to wait until the boys get back. They will find out for us.

Claudia: What if the baby really is the Messiah you are looking for? Maybe the shepherds heard the news that the angels sang and came looking for him. Do you think that is possible?

Lela: I don't know. It sure has been a strange night. Anything could happen if God decided to make it happen. I can't understand God sending the Messiah in the form of a little baby — especially one so poor. But God will be God and anything is possible. Listen! I hear the boys coming back.

(Cornelius and Adam enter.)

Adam: It was the shepherds, all right. They said they were watching their sheep when all of a sudden the sky was filled with light and singing and music and angels.

Susanna: See, I told you it was angels.

Cornelius: Yeah, they said the angels told them not to be afraid! But, I sure would have been afraid.

Adam: The angels told them that God has sent his own Son to earth — the Messiah. And he was born tonight.

Cornelius: Yeah, right here in Bethlehem. The angel told them they would find the baby wrapped in swaddling clothes, lying in a manger.

Lela: In a manger? You mean the manger we cleaned and fixed for Mary to lay her baby in? The baby in the stable is the Messiah?

Adam: That's what the shepherds said the angels told them. They were so excited and curious that they left their sheep to come and see what the angels had told them.

Cornelius: They were kneeling before the baby like ... like ... he was a King or something. *(Pause)* That's it! He is a King. He sure doesn't look like a King, but he must be one or the angels wouldn't have sent them here to see the baby in a manger!

Claudia: Let's go downstairs and tell Momma and Papa. This news is too good to keep to ourselves.

Susanna: Yes, let's go.

Lydia: *(Sits up, rubs her eyes again.)* Me too! I want to go, too.

Lela: Yes, you, too. Come on. Let's hurry!

(Children all exit as music begins to play "While Shepherds Watched Their Flocks By Night.")

Scene V

(The adults are all in one room with many others. Some are sitting around tables, some slouched in chairs, some curled up on the floor trying to sleep. Marcus, Portia, Miriam and Joshua are seated at a table where they are exchanging conversation about their different lifestyles.)

Portia: You mean you never eat pork and stuff like that!

Miriam: It is against our custom. Our God told Moses to tell us not to eat those kinds of things in order to stay healthy.

Marcus: What about this Messiah the kids were talking about? Is it true you look for a King to save you from our Roman government?

Joshua: Not really from your government, as much as from any oppression. We have been an oppressed people for a long time because we disobeyed God and even worshiped false gods.

Portia: You mean the gods we worship are false gods?

Miriam: They are for us. Our God has chosen us to be his people and many times our people have turned away from God.

Joshua: But, God loves us anyway and promised to send a King of all kings who would be a Savior for all people who are oppressed in any way.

Marcus: But won't that be treason?

Joshua: I don't know how it will work. But God will provide.

(Children all run in and gather close to their parents.)

Adam: *(Calling as he runs.)* Momma! Papa! Come quick. We have seen the Messiah!

Cornelius: Yes, I have seen him, too. Come, let us go to worship him like the shepherds did!

Lela: Can we go, too? Please? Can we?

Miriam: Messiah? Shepherds? What are you talking about? Why aren't you asleep?

Claudia: We heard music. It was beautiful. I thought it must be angels.

Susanna: No, I thought it was angels.

Adam: We all heard it. They sang about "peace on earth" and "good will to everyone." It really was beautiful.

Cornelius: Then it stopped. And the star is so bright we couldn't sleep anyway.

Adam: Then we saw these men coming into town. They headed for the stable and we were afraid for our baby.

Cornelius: So we, Adam and I, went to see what was going on.

Adam: They said the angels told them they would find the Messiah — God's own Son — wrapped in swaddling clothes, lying in a manger.

Joshua: In a manger? The Messiah?

Miriam: You mean we gave our room to the Messiah?

Portia: But, surely a King would be born in a palace with lots of fine clothes and a soft bed.

Miriam: Maybe, but our God loves us. It would be like our God to make the Messiah one of us so we would know he really understands our plight.

Lela: Can we go see, Momma? Can we worship, too?

Joshua: But, what of Mary, the mother? Don't you think she will be tired and need her rest?

Miriam: Joshua is right. We should not disturb her now.

Claudia: We will be very quiet. We may never have another chance to see the Messiah. Please, may we go?

Cornelius: She is right. We have already been touched by his birth. How can we be in the very presence of their God and not worship?

Marcus: Is that my son speaking?

Portia: He is right, you know. We have been changed because of the events of this night. We can go and just peek in. We will not stay.

Joshua: We will go, then. But, somehow, I do not believe we can just peek into the presence of God and go away unchanged. The children are right. We must go and worship. Let us go quickly and quietly.

Aaron: *(Enters as Joshua is finishing talking.)* Go where? It is late. Where are you going this time of night? Do you not like my generosity?

Miriam: We are going to the stable to see the baby that was born. Some shepherds came and said an angel told them the child is the Messiah.

Aaron: Messiah? In my stable? Bah! Humbug! Don't be foolish. When the Messiah comes we will know. He will be a King.

Lela: Even kings have to be born first, Uncle Aaron. Come with us and see.

Aaron: You all have taken leave of your senses! There is no Messiah. I wonder sometimes if there is even a God! No. Go if you will, but I have more sense than to run out into the dead of night to see a baby — one born in a stable yet! Ha! You are so foolish!

Lela: Uncle Aaron, did you ever hear an angel sing?

Aaron: Don't be foolish!

Joshua: Come, let us go. You know where to find us if you change your mind, my brother.

(All leave except Aaron, who stands shaking his head in disbelief. Then he leaves. Music begins to play "Silent Night.")

Scene VI

(Mary, Joseph and manger. Families enter quietly, children whispering among themselves, excitedly.)

Joseph: More visitors? Come in. Come in.

Joshua: We are sorry. We do not want to intrude. We do not want to disturb Mary and the baby. The children told us of the shepherds' visit and we wanted to worship the Messiah.

Mary: You have already worshiped.

Miriam: But, we have not been here.

Mary: You gave up your warmth and comfort for us. You made a bed for the King and you, Miriam, gave your very own swaddling clothes to wrap him in. And you, Marcus and Portia, gave up your comfort to make room for Joshua and his family. Yes, you have worshiped the Messiah already.

Joseph: She is right. To worship our God is to be open to the needs of God's people.

Marcus: But, we want to just gaze on the wonder of it all. Can we just kneel for a minute?

Joseph: Of course you can. Maybe we can hear again the angel's song. Maybe we can have "Peace on Earth!"

Mary: Yes . . . Peace on Earth. Although, I fear for the future.

Joshua: God will provide. Let us worship.

(All kneel around the manger. Aaron slips in unnoticed by the others. He looks toward the manger and begins to sing.)

Aaron: *(Singing)*

Chorus:
I have seen him, I have seen him;
I have seen the King, Messiah,
Emmanuel, God with us,
Prince of Peace and King of kings,
I have seen him,
I have seen the King, Messiah, Prince of Peace.

Verse 1:
See the child asleep in the manger
While we kneel here before him,
Oh, I wonder if he knows what lies ahead?
Gentle baby, our Messiah, in a manger bed.

Chorus:
I have seen him, I have seen him;
I have seen the King, Messiah,
Emmanuel, God with us.
Prince of Peace and King of kings,
I have seen him,
I have seen the King, Messiah, Prince of Peace!
I have seen the Prince of Peace!

(Speaking) I have seen the Prince of Peace!

(Walks over and picks up the baby, holding him gently, lovingly.)

Is it possible that I hold in my arms God's salvation? Is it possible that God loved us enough to do this for us?

(He is thoughtful for a moment.)

Yes, it is possible. I have seen the Messiah! I hold the Messiah but somehow, I believe the Messiah holds me.

(Lays the baby back in the manger, turns to the rest.)

Come, we must let the Holy Family rest. I have a feeling they will need it before the world is through with them!

(All leave looking at Aaron with awe and disbelief. Aaron, Cornelius, Adam and Lela are last to leave.)

Cornelius: Is that your uncle?

Adam: Yes. Remember Papa said we could not be in the presence of God without it making a difference.

Lela: I sure hope it makes a difference to the world. I wish I could see the future.

Adam: I'm not sure we would really want to, but for now, we can tell everyone we meet that the Messiah is here. They will not believe us, but we will know. And some day, who knows, maybe our paths will cross again.

(Aaron is the last to leave. He turns once more and looks toward the holy family.)

Aaron: There has been a miracle in Bethlehem this night which will shatter the world! May God give you strength to endure. May God's Peace reign forever more.

(He turns and walks slowly away.)

Congregation: "Joy To The World."

I have Seen him

Adagio ♩ = 72   **Mary Lu Warstler**

(Chorus) *mp*   I have seen   him,   I have seen   him,

I have seen   the   king Mes - si -   ah;

E - man - u - al, God with us, Prince of Peace and

King of kings,   I have seen   him, I have seen the

(Second time to Coda)

King, Mes - si - ah, Prince of   Peace.

(Verse) *mp* See the child a - sleep in the man - ger,

While we are kneeling here be - fore him?

Oh, I won - der if he knows what lies a - head;

Gen - tle Ba - by, our Mes - si - ah in a

(Repeat Chorus)

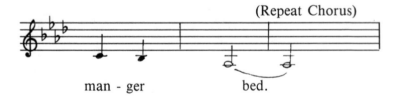

man - ger bed.

Coda

I have seen the Prince of Peace.